Table of Contents

INTRODUCTION

Becoming a millionaire is not a goal that can be achieved overnight for most people. In fact, many of the world's richest people built their wealth over many years (sometimes even generations) by making smart but often bold decisions, putting their skills to the best use possible, and doggedly pursuing their vision. If you can learn anything about millionaires, it's that for many of them, their riches are not necessarily what most sets them apart from the rest of the world—it's what they did to earn those millions that really stands out.

5 SIMPLE HABITS OF THE AVERAGE MILLIONAIRE

1. They're avid readers.

President Harry Truman once said, "Not all readers are leaders, but all leaders are readers." One of the reasons millionaires become millionaires is because of their constant desire to learn. To them, leadership books and biographies are much more important than the latest reality show or who got kicked off the island. When they have free time, they use it wisely—by reading.

2. They understand delayed gratification.

Millionaires spend most of their lives sacrificing temporary pleasures for long-term success. They have no problem buying an older used car, living in a modest neighborhood and wearing inexpensive clothes. They don't care about keeping up with the Joneses. Millionaires spend most of their lives sacrificing temporary pleasures for long-term success. These decisions allow them to do things like save for retirement and college, and build up a large down payment for their dream home. They realize that instant gratification is fun—but delayed gratification is so much better. Today's sacrifices set them up for tomorrow's success.

3. They stay away from debt.

One of the biggest myths out there is that average millionaires see "debt as a tool." Not true. If they want something they can't afford, they save and pay cash for it later. Be confident about your retirement. Find an investing pro in your area today.

Car payments, student loans, same-as-cash financing plans—these just aren't part of their vocabulary. That's why they win with money. They don't owe anything to the bank, so every dollar they earn stays with them to spend, save and give! Debt is the biggest obstacle to building wealth. We tell that to everyone. You need to avoid it like the plague. Your dreams are too important!

4. They budget.

Your budget is your plan. And you can't build a million-dollar net worth without a plan, people. Success isn't an accident. You are in charge of your own wealth-building. You can't build a million-dollar net worth without a plan. Just like you build a house by starting with the foundation, you build wealth by starting with the budgeting basics. And then you keep following them. When you're making a lot of money, you don't stop managing it, right? Average millionaires have made a habit of budgeting every month. They know what's coming in and what's leaving their bank accounts. If you only remember one thing, it should be this: Budgeting is the key to winning with money. It's telling each dollar where to go at the beginning of the month instead of wondering where it all went.

5. They give.

Sure, some rich people can be selfish jerks—just like anyone else. But the millionaires who live down the street, the ones you don't even realize are wealthy, are some of the most giving people you'll ever meet. We know because we've met a lot of them. They work hard, save and respect the ability of others to do the same.

How Can You Tell If Someone Is a Millionaire?

For most Americans, achieving millionaire status may be more realistic. The Global Wealth Report 2022, produced by the Credit Suisse Research Institute, notes that there were 24,480 millionaires in the country as of 2021. But to become a millionaire, you need a millionaire mindset. If you are ready to join the tens of thousands of people who have money in the bank and substantial assets to their names, then you need to know how they think as well as how they invest and spend their money. Luckily, there are a few things that most wealthy people do that can help you understand millionaires a little better. Here are eight subtle ways you can tell that someone is a millionaire.

They Value Their Time

One thing that sets millionaires apart is that they always place a high value on their time. Many quiet millionaires are surprisingly frugal, but they do not mind spending money on things that will save them time. They may hire a driver so that they can work during their morning commute or have a personal assistant to help them manage everything they have going on.

They Don't Talk About Money

Another tell-tale sign of a millionaire is that they don't talk about money. They generally shy away from conversations about how much money they make or what assets they have. People who are genuinely wealthy usually do not like to discuss it. They don't usually feel the need to show their wealth through flashy fashion or by bragging about their material items. Most of the time, millionaires are investors, but they don't blab about their investments. They keep quiet about what has made them money but continue to acquire wealth throughout their lifetimes.

Their Things Are Customized

While most millionaires aren't interested in wearing head-to-toe logos, they do usually opt to have their clothing tailored. They also don't mind spending more on customized furniture, cars and homes. Most people who have acquired some amount of wealth focus on quality instead of quantity. Their wardrobes tend to be classic and timeless. Their houses tend to be minimalistic but filled with high-quality pieces.

They Own Multiple Properties

An undeniable sign that you are in the presence of a millionaire is that they own multiple properties. Real estate can be a great investment, but the average person usually can't afford to buy more than one house. Millionaires, on the other hand, may have the means to purchase a vacation home or rental property. They may not talk about it, but if you pay attention, they may let it slip that they have a home in the Hamptons or Palm Springs.

They Have an Expensive Hobby

If you meet someone that mentions yachting, fencing or golfing, you might be talking to a millionaire. Wealthy people frequently indulge in costly hobbies, and it isn't just an occasional outing. Millionaires don't just go golfing with friends, they belong to country clubs. They don't just rent a boat, they own a yacht. While wealthy people may not always flaunt their money, they do like to make time for things that bring them happiness.

They Are Well-Traveled

Millionaires tend to be well-traveled. They traverse the globe immersing themselves in other cultures. They also may take longer vacations than most, spending a few weeks away or having no problem jetting off for just the weekend. As with their clothing and furniture, their travel is usually customized. Their itineraries are tailored to their specific needs, and they do not mind going private to get them to their destinations quickly.

They Can Speak Multiple Languages

If your newest acquaintance casually mentions that they can speak multiple languages, they might just be wealthier than you think. Millionaires may need to know how to speak another language for their business, or they may have simply wanted to learn it to keep pace on their travels.

Either way, the ability to speak more than one language comes in handy in their everyday lives.

The Keep a Close Circle

A final clue that a millionaire is a millionaire is the friends they keep. People with money tend to keep smaller friend groups. They may know a lot of people but only allow a limited number to get close. They keep their circle small in an effort to protect themselves and their family from scrutiny.

6 MILLIONAIRE TRAITS THAT YOU CAN ADOPT

Millionaires have more in common with each other than just their bank accounts—for some millionaires, striking it rich took courage, salesmanship, vision, and passion. Find out which traits are most common among the seven-figure bank account set and what you can do to build some of these skills yourself.

1. Independent Thinking

Millionaires think differently. Not just about money, about everything. The time and energy everybody else spends attempting to conform, millionaires spend creating their own path. Since thoughts impact actions, people who want to be wealthy should think in a way that will get them to that goal. Independent thinking doesn't mean doing the opposite of what the rest of the world is doing; it means having the courage to follow what is important to you. So, the lesson here is to forge your own way. Let your success drive you to financial spoils rather than doing it the other way around and trying to chase the money.

For example, David Geffen is a self-made millionaire with $9.9 billion to his name in 2021, according to Forbes. This American record executive and film producer was a college dropout, but Geffen made millions by founding record agencies, including DreamWorks Animation SKG Inc., and signed some of the most prominent musicians of the '70s and '80s. Although he didn't take what many assume to be the usual path to success, his tireless work ethic and sense of personal conviction about artists' potential allowed him to rack up a sizable fortune.

2. Vision

Millionaires are creative visionaries with a positive attitude. In other words, wealthy people have big dreams, and they believe they will come true. As such, wealth seekers should set lofty goals and not be afraid of uncharted territory. Bill Gates, the world's second-richest person in 2021 with a net worth of $124 billion, according to Forbes, did just that. The co-founder of Microsoft (NYSE: MSFT) brought personal computers to the masses. Gates jumped into the personal computers business in 1975 and held on tight, creating Microsoft Windows in 1985. When consumers began to bring computers into their homes, Gates was ready to profit from this new age.

In mid-March 2020, Gates stepped down as a board member of Microsoft. He co-chairs the Bill & Melinda Gates Foundation, the world's largest private charitable foundation to which the couple has donated $35.8 billion worth of Microsoft stock. Gates is also now a staunch spokesperson and scholar on the subject of climate change.

3. Skills

Millionaires also tend to partner with others to supplement their weaker skills. If you don't know what you are good at, poll friends and family. Use training and mentors to refine your strong skills.

4. Passion

Billionaire investing guru Warren Buffett says, "Money is a by-product of something I like to do very much." Enjoying your work allows you to have the discipline to work hard at it every day. People who interact with money for a living, bankers, for example, often love creating new deals and persuading others to complete a transaction.

But finding your dream job may take time, and becoming a millionaire takes time. According to Entrepreneur, even the wealthiest millionaires took an average of eight years to earn their first million. Not only that, but many experience significant failure along the way. Pavle Marinkovic, writing for Medium.com, shows that Warren Buffett, Steve Ballmer, former Microsoft CEO, and Rupert Murdoch of the Fox media empire, all made huge mistakes before they were successful. So, if you want to be rich, stop doing things you don't enjoy, and do what you love. If you don't know what you love, try a few things and keep trying until you hit on the right thing.

5. Investment

Millionaires are willing to sacrifice time and money to achieve their goals. They are willing to take a risk now for the opportunity of achieving something greater in the future. Investing may include securities or starting a business— either way, it is a step toward achieving great financial rewards. Start investing now.

6. Salesmanship

Millionaires are constantly presenting their ideas and persuading others to buy into them. Good salesmen are oblivious to critics and naysayers. In other words, they don't take no for an answer. Millionaires also have good social skills. In fact, when writer T. Harv Eker analyzed the results of a survey of 753 millionaires for his book, Secrets of the Millionaire Mind (2005), he found social skills were more important than IQ. The ability to communicate with people is essential to selling your idea. Contrary to the traditional view of salesmen, millionaires cite honesty as an important factor in their success. If you want to be a millionaire, be an honest salesman, and polish your social skills.

Decamillionaire: Definition, Word Origin, Uses

Decamillionaire is a term used for someone with a net worth of over 10 million of a given currency, most often U.S. dollars, euros, or pounds sterling. The term decamillionaire is made up of two words, "deca" and "millionaire." The word "deca" or "deka" is of Greek origin, meaning ten. The International System of Units (SI) also defines the prefix "deca" as ten. While the word millionaire is used for someone whose net worth or wealth is equal to or more than a million (1,000,000). When we combine these two to reflect the wealth of a person, it becomes 'ten times a million,' which mathematically works out as 10 x 1,000,000 = 10,000,000. The term is most often used as a benchmark for wealth in countries with currencies that compare to the value of the U.S. dollar, euro or British pound sterling.

Understanding Decamillionaire
A person who has 2.5 million in a given currency can be called a multimillionaire, and so can somebody who has 10 million. While the first one has '2.5 times a million,' the

second one has '10 times a million,' which is a sizable difference not well represented by the traditional net-worth categorizations. Thus, the term decamillionaire is used to reflect the size of one's wealth more precisely.

Decamillionaires and Net Worth

Often, wealthy individuals are clubbed together in the category of 'millionaires' or 'multimillionaires,' but this segregation is too broad to describe a person's wealth accurately. Some wealth management firms further categorize wealthy individuals or families as "high-net-worth,""very-high-net-worth," or "ultra-high-net-worth." For the sake of simplicity, U.S. dollars will be used to provide a guide to how much wealth qualifies an individual for each of these categories. A high-net-worth individual is one with at least $1 million in investable assets (such as equities and bonds) excluding their primary residence. Different banks or wealth management firms may have their own definitions or thresholds, however. A very-high net worth individual is one with at least $5 million in investable assets, sometimes referred to as a "pentamillionaire." Meanwhile, an ultra-high-net-worth individual is one with at least $30 million to invest. As of 2016, there were just over 73,000 ultra-high-net-worth individuals in the United States.

Decamillionare Use

Given how broad these definitions are, terms like decamillionaire are used to provide a more accurate snapshot of individual wealth. With the ever-increasing number of millionaires the world over, and with the effect of inflation on buying power of their wealth, terms like decamillionaire are used to delineate simple millionaires from those with multiple times the amount of wealth.

7 Dos and Don'ts for Becoming a Billionaire

Becoming a billionaire is a lofty goal, often unobtainable for most individuals. Some find their success through economic, educational, or opportunistic advantages. Others learn to take calculated risks, develop their personal creativity, and deploy their capital advantageously. On the other hand, some miss out on the opportunity for wealth because they do not have a long-term plan or try to rush success. By leveraging focus, discipline, and routine frameworks, you can increase your likelihood of financial success. Here are some specific do's and don't for becoming a billionaire.

Do: Invent

Inventing is a challenging career path to take. But if you've got the smarts to create successfully, patent, produce and market a product that people need (and thus, will buy in droves), you can build your future billionaire life on it. Successful inventions aren't necessarily complicated or high-tech items but can improve existing items. For example, James Dyson invented a better vacuum cleaner, and Gianfranco Zaccai invented a better mop, the Swiffer.

Do: Innovate

Innovation is the fine art of considering a current mainstream market and finding a creative way to improve the current offering. Successful innovators will identify the real needs behind customer demands and meet them with a smarter, better, more efficient product or service that provides more than its competitors. Others may develop a business that works in a way just different enough to stand out from the rest. IKEA founder Ingvar Kamprad is an excellent example of someone who used innovation to yield billions.

Furniture doesn't seem like a fascinating market. Still, his approach of providing modular, economical pieces with a modern flair from Sweden and other European designers and manufacturers to a global market proved fruitful.

Do: Invest

Self-made billionaire Warren Buffett is famous for his frugal ways and smart investments. Investing, of course, requires a little seed money and some accurate insight into which investments are smart and which could result in a loss. If you can follow in the footsteps of billionaire investors like Buffett, then this might be the route for you.

Do: Be an Entrepreneur

The third option for becoming a billionaire is the time-honored tradition of entrepreneurial pursuits. Starting a business and taking it to success isn't always easy. Still, for those with good business sense and the ability to spot startups that have the potential to be great, entrepreneurship can be the vehicle to great wealth. Billionaire entrepreneurs might work in one of two ways: either by coming up with a great idea and taking it all the way, as in the case of Bill Gates and Microsoft, or by spotting someone else's good idea and investing in it early on. Both are viable ways to reach the success that can get you billions of dollars for your net worth. Long-term holdings in the stock market may be a better bet than popular high-risk investments, according to billionaire Warren Buffett.

Don't: Think You Know It All

The moment you think you have nothing left to learn is the moment you kill your potential for becoming a billionaire. Especially if you're interested in building your wealth through inventing or innovating, you have to be curious, open-minded, and always learning. Those qualities allow you to look at old things in a new way, to see the potential for change and profit where others see only what already had been done.

Don't: Make Flashy Investments

The latest and greatest investment opportunity may be fun to talk about, but one of the pitfalls of would-be billionaires is to jump in on the "next big thing," which doesn't always turn out to be so big. Investors who make billions from their investments avoid flashy, fun, and high-risk picks and instead choose those with long-term potential to provide great returns. Real estate, energy, steel, telecommunications, pharmaceuticals, and energy are among the picks, while high-tech and intriguing but risky options may go either way.

Don't: Quit Too Soon

Entrepreneurial types who succeed realize that success rarely comes overnight. One business idea might not pay off, but the next might. It's not easy to build something from scratch, especially when your something is a fortune of billions. Time is on your side if you don't rush it.

How Can I Become a Billionaire?

It isn't easy to become a billionaire especially if you haven't already made millions. You will need time, patience, investment savvy, and entrepreneurship to become a billionaire unless you are born into a family with billions that you stand to inherit. Who Was the First Billionaire?

John D. Rockefeller may have been America's first billionaire, as reported in 1916. However, there are historians who argue this fact, stating Rockefeller came close but did not achieve the status of a billionaire. Some say Henry Ford earned the title.

How to Reach Financial Freedom: 12 Habits to Get You There

Financial freedom—having enough savings, investments, and cash on hand to afford the lifestyle you want for yourself and your family— is an important goal for many people. It also means growing a nest egg that will allow you to retire or pursue any career you want—without being driven by the need to earn a certain amount each year. Unfortunately, too many people fall far short of financial freedom. Even without occasional financial emergencies, escalating debt due to overspending is a constant burden that keeps them from reaching their goals. When a major crisis—such as a hurricane, an earthquake, or a pandemic—completely disrupts all plans, additional holes in safety nets are revealed. Trouble happens to nearly everyone, but these 12 habits can put you on the right path. Being financially independent means having sufficient income, savings, or investments to live comfortably for life and meet all of one's obligations without relying on a paycheck. That is the ultimate goal of a long-term financial plan.

1. Set Life Goals

What is financial freedom to you? Everyone has a general desire for it, but that's too vague a goal. You need to get specific about amounts and deadlines. The more specific your goals, the higher the likelihood of achieving them. Write down these three objectives:

What your lifestyle requires

How much you should have in your bank account to make that possible

What age is the deadline to save that amount

Next, count backward from your deadline age to your current age and establish financial mileposts at regular intervals between the two dates. Write all amounts and deadlines down carefully and put the goal sheet at the front of your financial binder.

2. Make a Monthly Budget

Making a monthly household budget—and sticking to it—is the best way to guarantee that all bills are paid and savings are on track. It's also a regular routine that reinforces your goals and bolsters resolve against the temptation to splurge.

3. Pay off Credit Cards in Full

Credit cards and other high-interest consumer loans are toxic to wealth-building. Make it a point to pay off the full balance each month. Student loans, mortgages, and similar loans typically have much lower interest rates; paying them off is not an emergency. However, paying these lower-interest loans on time is still important—and on-time payments will build a good credit rating.

4. Create Automatic Savings

Pay yourself first. Enroll in your employer's retirement plan and make full use of any matching contribution benefit, which is essentially free money. It's also wise to have an automatic withdrawal into an emergency fund, which can be tapped for unexpected expenses, as well as an automatic contribution to a brokerage account or something similar. Ideally, the money for the emergency fund and the retirement fund should be pulled out of your account the same day you receive your paycheck, so it never even touches your hands.

Keep in mind that the recommended amount to save in an emergency fund depends on your individual circumstances. Also, tax-advantaged retirement accounts come with rules that make it difficult to get your hands on your cash should you suddenly need it, so that account should not be your only emergency fund.

5. Start Investing Now

Bad stock markets—known as bear markets—can make people question the wisdom of investing, but historically there has been no better way to grow your money. The magic of compound interest alone will grow your money exponentially, but you do need a lot of time to achieve meaningful growth. However, remember that—for everyone except professional investors—it would be a mistake to attempt the kind of stock picking made famous by billionaires like Warren Buffett. Instead, open an online brokerage account that makes it easy for you to learn how to invest, create a manageable portfolio, and make weekly or monthly contributions to it automatically. We've ranked the best online brokers for beginners to help you get started.

Achieving financial freedom can be very difficult in the face of growing debt, cash emergencies, medical issues, and overspending, but—with discipline and careful planning—it is possible. That is the ultimate goal of

6. Watch Your Credit Score

Your credit score is a very important number that determines the interest rate you are offered when buying a new car or refinancing a home. It also impacts the amount you pay for a range other essentials, from car insurance to life insurance premiums.

The reason credit scores have so much weight is that someone with reckless financial habits is considered likely to be reckless in other areas of life, such as not looking after their health—or even driving and drinking. This is why it's important to get a credit report at regular intervals to make sure that there are no erroneous black marks ruining your good name. It may also be worth looking into a reputable credit monitoring service to protect your information.

7. Negotiate for Goods and Services

Many Americans are hesitant to negotiate for goods and services, because they're afraid that it makes them seem cheap. Conquer this fear and you could save thousands each year. Small businesses, in particular, tend to be open to negotiation, so buying in bulk or positioning yourself as a repeat customer can open the door to good discounts.

8. Stay Educated on Financial Issues

Review relevant changes in tax law to ensure that all adjustments and deductions are maximized each year. Keep up with financial news and developments in the stock market and do not hesitate to adjust your investment portfolio accordingly. Knowledge is also the best defense against fraudsters who prey on unsophisticated investors to turn a quick buck.

9. Maintain Your Property

Taking good care of property makes everything from cars and lawnmowers to shoes and clothes last longer. The cost of maintenance is a fraction of the cost of replacement, so it's an investment not to be missed.

10. Live Below Your Means

Mastering a frugal lifestyle means developing a mindset focused on living a good life with less—and it's easier than you think. In fact, before rising to affluence, many wealthy individuals developed the habit of living below their means. This isn't a challenge to adopt a minimalist lifestyle. It simply means learning to distinguish between the things you need and the things you want—and then making small adjustments that drive big gains for your financial health.

11. Get a Financial Advisor

Once you've gotten to a point where you've amassed a decent amount of wealth—either liquid assets (cash or anything easily converted to cash) or fixed assets (property or anything not easily converted to cash)—get a financial advisor to help you stay on the right path.

12. Take Care of Your Health

The principle of proper maintenance also applies to your body—and taking excellent care of your physical health has a significant positive impact on your financial health as well. Investing in good health is not difficult. It means making regular visits to doctors and dentists, and following health advice about any problems you encounter. Many medical issues can be helped—or even prevented—with basic lifestyle changes, such as more exercise and a healthier diet. Poor health maintenance, on the other hand, has both immediate and long-term negative consequences on your financial goals. Some companies have limited sick days, which means a loss of income once paid days are used up. Obesity and other dietary illnesses make insurance premiums skyrocket, and poor health may force early retirement with lower monthly income for the rest of your life.

What Is Financial Freedom?

Everyone defines financial freedom in terms of their own goals. For most people, it means having the financial cushion (savings, investments, and cash) to afford a certain lifestyle—plus a nest egg for retirement or the freedom to pursue any career without the need to earn a certain salary.

The 50/30/20 budget rule, popularized by Senator Elizabeth Warren, is a guideline to achieve financial stability by dividing after-tax income into 3 categories of spending: 50% for needs, 30% for wants, and 20% for savings and paying down debt. We have built an easy-to-follow budgeting calculator to help you categorize and control your spending and saving—which is the essential first step toward financial freedom. Although some states—including California, Hawaii, Washington, Massachusetts, and Michigan—limit or prohibit the use of credit scores to determine auto insurance rates, many companies do use a credit-based scoring system to decide whether to insure you and how much you will pay.

These 12 steps won't solve all your money problems, but they will help you develop the good habits that get you on the path to financial freedom. Simply making a plan with specific target amounts and dates reinforces your resolve to reach your goal and guards you against the temptation to overspend. Once you start to make real progress, relief from the constant pressure of escalating debt and the promise of a nest egg for retirement kick in as powerful motivators—and financial freedom is in your sights.

How to become a millionaire by 30

We've all dreamt of countless holidays to far-away destinations and splashing the cash on the luxuries we've always wanted. But, the chances are you're resigned to this never becoming more than a daydream. However, becoming a millionaire isn't as difficult as you might think. Lots of people prove each year that you don't have to be a banker, lottery winner or be born with a silver spoon in your mouth to build up your wealth to seven figures. So, here's our ultimate guide to getting your hands on that million by 30. Let's get rich!

What makes a millionaire?

Let's start with a bit of a disclaimer: a million pounds just isn't what it used to be. It's getting easier to become a millionaire with every day that passes, thanks to things like inflation. And for many budding rich-listers, being wealthy is more a question of lifestyle and not having to worry about your finances, than the number in your bank account. To live like a millionaire, you don't actually need to have a million pounds in the bank. 99% of 'millionaires' don't. But to actually be a millionaire, you'll have to be on top of your finances and investments!

Being a millionaire can mean all sorts of things. In this guide, we're essentially going to map out a realistic path to building up your wealth beyond £1,000,000. We've suggested a few 'quick' ways to become a millionaire at the end for those who just can't wait... but stick with us for the foolproof guide first!

How to become a millionaire

Here are our top tips for becoming a millionaire:

Set goals

red pen ticking boxes

Credit: Kenishirotie – Shutterstock

The money game is a long slog – cash doesn't grow on trees. Before you embark on your millionaire challenge, it's vital that you have a clear life plan. If you're serious about this then you need to know how to achieve it, not just dream it! You need to work out a feasible and realistic route to making your millions. When doing so, draw on your skills, experience and ambitions. When it comes to setting income goals, think about when you'd like to retire. Most retirees are 'pensioners' because they're living off of their pension which at least covers living costs. But you want to live like a millionaire, right?

To get to this level of income without working requires a fairly sizeable pension, plus a good number of other streams of passive income being earned every month on your capital assets. If you want to really live it up post-work, set an income goal before you retire that doesn't require you to work anymore. This number will vary for everyone, but whatever it is, pick one and work to it. Instead of retiring at 70, you might find you're able to retire at 58 because you've reached your goal. By the time you give up work, your investment portfolio becomes your income portfolio. We go into more detail about how investing will help you become a millionaire below.

Budget every month

Practising some basic budgeting and money-saving skills as soon as possible will stand you in good stead for the rest of your life. Don't just write it off as 'something you'll do another day'! If you haven't already got it, download our free Student Money Cheat Sheet. There are loads of great tips in there to get you started. Sticking to your budget takes discipline, but the sooner you get into the millionaire mindset of buying assets instead of liabilities, the better. Most millionaires don't run around buying Lamborghinis all the time while cracking open the champagne at breakfast.

In fact, that's part of the reason why they're millionaires in the first place. Instead of splashing the cash at every given opportunity, they've allowed their money to grow. They say that "a fool and his cash are soon parted", and that's a fairly decent motto to live by if you want to join the super-rich.

Start as soon as possible

Time is a valuable asset, especially when it comes to saving and investing money. So the sooner you start, the better chances you have of becoming a millionaire. Use any spare time you have (aside from studying and partying) to earn some cash. It's a good idea to land a part-time job, but it can also pay off to be more creative.

Or why not start up a small business of your own if you have something to offer? Not only will this pull in some additional cash, but you'll be testing out your entrepreneurial skills before you've even graduated. There's no avoiding the fact you'll have to repay your Student Loan, but not straight away (if ever). It's not like other debt and won't affect your future goals of raking in the big bucks. And you might find that sometimes you do have a few quid to spare, especially when the loans come in. Get into the habit of putting this into the savings account that makes the most financial sense to you (easy access is best at this stage). You'll be surprised how much interest you can earn on it during your time at uni. At the same time, remember to cut down on spending. Avoid having a car and think carefully before splashing out on big-ticket items if you don't really need them.

Put money in a tax-free ISA

One of the reasons why people will never become millionaires is simply because they don't know how to. There are lots of competing options out there fighting for you to invest in. You need to think smart and do your homework on what's available to you and what will give you the best return. In the UK, tax-free cash ISAs are one of the best ways to consistently build up your savings.

Why get a tax-free cash ISA?

Every year, each person in the UK over the age of 16 has an allowance of money (£20,000 maximum) they can put in a tax-free savings account, called an ISA. Once your money's in the account, it stays tax-free, FOREVER. If you don't use up your ISA allowance in a particular year, you lose that opportunity. So if you've got a bit of spare money lying around, it's worth thinking about putting it in an ISA.

You can move to a different ISA provider every year if you want to, so shop around for the best rate. The top interest rates are usually a couple of percent. So, if you deposit

£20,000 in one of the best ISAs, you'll earn a few hundred quid over the year in tax-free interest.

You may argue that basic-rate taxpayers get £1,000 of interest tax-free each year, so there's no point in opening an ISA right now. Indeed, if a basic-rate taxpayer chose to invest £20,000 in a 2% savings account instead of an ISA with the same interest rate, they'd still receive £400. But this tip isn't for the here and now – it's for the future. Say you sell your business, or get a significant pay rise. All of a sudden you're not a basic-rate taxpayer, and your tax-free interest allowance drops to £500 or possibly nothing, depending on your earnings. All that interest you're earning is going to be taxed in a big way. So, given that there are no real disadvantages to keeping your money in an ISA instead of a regular savings account, and some fairly significant advantages, we'd say it's a no-brainer.

Invest in yourself

One of the most profitable investments you'll ever make is investing in yourself. And we don't mean getting the most expensive haircuts and designer outfits. We mean investing in your skills, mindset and knowledge. Developing your skills can help you climb the corporate ladder and create passive income streams outside of your job. Plus, working on your mindset and knowledge around money lets you make better financial decisions that will set you up for a better future. We have a list of books about money to get you started. And don't forget to look after your body and mind. Creating financial freedom is fantastic, but if your physical and mental health is suffering, it's hard to enjoy the millionaire lifestyle.

Work in an industry that you love and pays well

In order to maximise your income, you should try to secure a well-paid graduate job. Having said that, think carefully about the career you want to embark on: one you will enjoy and can progress quickly in. Graduate schemes are often the best way to kick off your career on a high earner early on. Many companies offer graduate salaries of £40,000 a year (if not more)! If you're finding it hard to get on the career ladder, get a part-time role for the time being while you job hunt. And, if you're really struggling to find any paid work, don't be afraid to sign on at the Job Centre for a short period.

Start your own business

The fast-track method of becoming rich in your twenties is to start a high-growth, high-return business with a plan to exit within five years or so. But, of course, there's absolutely no guarantee you'll even make a penny, and the risk can often outweigh your other options for building a long-term income. It's important to have a well-researched idea and a solid business plan before you start, as well as a clear picture of how you'll support yourself when there's no money coming in. Having said all this, there may never be a better time to start in business than as a graduate. Your responsibilities are minimal and even if it all goes wrong, you've got a wealth of experience to build on and take forward.

Diversify your income and investments

Never keep all your eggs in one basket. Over the years, you should aim to build up a portfolio of wise investments that will get you set for when you retire. A good income portfolio would ideally include a mix of:

Cash and stock ISAs

Government bonds

A pension (private or state)

Index-tracker funds

Buy-to-let property (UK or overseas)

Cash.

All of these are sources of sustained income. This kind of balanced portfolio will leave you in a position to enjoy your retirement, rather than wondering how you'll afford it. And with the UK's state pension getting worse each year, that's a very good position to be in!

WHAT ARE THE BENEFITS OF BUYING A PROPERTY?

Once you've bought your first house or flat, you'll probably be paying much less every month in mortgage repayments than you had been forking out on rent. And you actually have a place of your very own at the end of it. Historically, property prices follow a strong upward trend so you really are investing in your future. If you're in a good financial position, then considering a buy-to-let investment is the next step to financial freedom.

So long as you can get the initial deposit down and get a good mortgage deal that is less than the rental income, you're on the fast track to being rather rich. Again, you're likely to benefit from a rise in overall property prices. This means you can bring in big bucks by selling at the peak of the market and buying at the bottom. Of course, there is the whole issue of getting a deposit together, and that's a lot easier said than done. But the budgeting skills you honed as a student will help you put a plan in place to save up the necessary amount.

Get to grips with your pension

Retirement might seem like a long way off yet. But, sorting out a pension fund before you hit 30 is a very wise move. The benefits of pensions in growing your wealth are on a par with index-tracker investments. Even putting a modest amount into a pension fund now can make a big difference in the future. Remember, time is crucial if you want to reap the benefits of compound interest. As with many of the other tips on this page, the key thing is to grow your knowledge of these major types of investment products available to you.

If you're employed, you may receive a workplace pension. If so, ask for details about the provider, as you're free to opt for a better or cheaper plan elsewhere.

Tips to Increase Your Net Worth

Your net worth can tell you many things, but it is simply a way to gauge your own financial success. Many have calculated their net worth and come to the conclusion that it is in need of a revamp, yet improving it can seem very difficult. However, it only requires some guidance, a little willpower, and a lot of patience.

Pay Off Your Debt

The money you owe is money that could be used to grow your net worth. Pay off all your debt as soon as you are able, but be aware of penalties that can be applied for early payment (like with mortgages). Consolidating your debt by taking out a loan at a lower rate to pay down high-yield debt is a tried and true strategy. The bottom line here is to know what you owe and have a plan for paying it back. Make extra payments where possible and work to reduce your overall debt burden.

Max Out Your Retirement Contributions

Many private employers provide retirement plans that have desirable tax characteristics. Other tax-advantaged accounts (ex. a Roth IRA) are also available. In fact, many employers have matching programs that will help you grow your contribution faster. By not taking advantage of such programs, you are leaving money on the table. Retirement contributions create a two-fold benefit. They defer your taxable income to your lowest earning years and increase your available generative assets. Taking action now for your retirement will help slow one of the biggest impediments to the growth of your net worth: taxes.

Cut Expenses By Realizing Expenses

Nobody likes to hear that they spend too much and need to cut back. We all know that eating out at restaurants or buying the latest gadgets catches up with us, but what we don't realize is how quickly smaller expenses can add up, too. Make a habit of noting your expenses every day for a week and you will be shocked by how much of your paycheck is trickling away. The intent is not to stop eating out or quit hobbies entirely, but instead to become aware of your spending habits and identify areas where you can make adjustments; a little goes a long way. In addition, remember that debt from step one? A large bulk of that comes from credit cards. Cutting up your credit cards and using only the cash you have available will help to curb your spending.

Keep Money You Have Saved Where It Will Grow

You probably already have a savings account, but are you using it? Your checking account should be lean enough for your regular spending and everything else should be in interest-bearing accounts. Even better, invest what you can. Some people tend to be risk-averse, so take a look at guaranteed investment contracts (GICs) or bond funds. If your savings are in a coffee tin above the fridge, you are not making your money work for you and are undermining your hard work. As a side note, resist the urge to immediately spend any windfalls you may receive; invest it to ensure that you will continue to reap the benefits well into the future.

Buy the Car You Will Drive Forever

It can be practically guaranteed that a vehicle purchased today will be worth much less in one year's time. Couple this depreciation with maintenance costs and insurance premiums and you have a recipe for the true financial cost of owning a car. Every new car you buy ultimately decreases your net worth. You can reduce the negative financial effects of owning an automobile by purchasing only the vehicle (or vehicles) you need, with an eye to driving it until it needs to be replaced.

Talk to a Professional

This is the most important step and yet the most overlooked. People don't want to pay to consult an accountant or financial advisor often because they are embarrassed about the state of their finances. With that said, talking to a professional can get you the latest information on how to utilize tax breaks or assist you in your budgeting. Never be ashamed to ask for help and use the resources that are available.

6 pro tips to achieving the millionaire mindset

A millionaire mindset is not actually about making a million dollars. It's not even about your net worth, living in a penthouse in New York, real estate, financial security, or your bank account.

To those who swear by it, a millionaire mindset is about focusing on changing your life — starting with your perspective — to accomplish the goals you've always dreamed of achieving. It's no small task, either. You must encourage purposeful habits and ways of thinking daily. The idea is that millionaires live in a place of abundance that lets them experience greater success and confidence. If you want to achieve your goals, you start by behaving as if you already have. In that space, your success fuels more success.

What are the habits of a millionaire mindset?

What do you have to do to have a millionaire mindset? Here are 10 habits of "millionaire thinking" for you to try out:

1. Focus on your goals

If you don't have your goals on your mind, how are you supposed to reach them? Your goals could be financial growth, more robust well-being, a particular career path, or any other dream. Make a habit of thinking about what you want to achieve. (On average, forming a habit takes 66 days.) Once you have your goals in mind, write them down and keep them where you'll see them often. They'll always be there to remind you what you're working for, even on tough days.

2. Get comfortable with always learning

People often need to remember that the world always offers you something to be a beginner at and start fresh. When working toward objectives, you may have to switch up strategies. Learning to adapt to constantly new changes might help you realize that your practices weren't beneficial before. Small skills help as well. Take note of all the new skills you learn and be proud of how you've continued to push forward.

3. Put yourself out there

You can't achieve your goals by never leaving the house or talking to anyone. Networking and paying attention to how you present yourself are essential. If you're trying out a business pitch, you need to be confident while expressing your passion. People recognize and remember bold, passionate, and courageous individuals speaking about their goals. Networking can help you connect with like-minded individuals who share the same drive as you. Making friends at work also turns colleagues into peers, which increases employee engagement.

4. Be patient

It can be frustrating to feel like you're hustling without being rewarded, but don't let this deter you from focusing on what you want in life. You can't change your life in a week. It's okay if you don't meet your personal development goals when you'd hoped. Good things take time, and just because things don't always happen when you want them to doesn't mean they never will.

5. Accept mistakes as they come

To grow and learn, you have to make mistakes. You shouldn't look at mistakes as things to avoid at all costs, but instead, as opportunities to learn from. Remember, too, that there's a difference between sloppy mistakes (avoid these) and plans that don't work out but give you more information and insight to try a new tactic. Failures are opportunities to learn about yourself and your team and offer a great way to develop new skills for the future. Instead of dwelling on your mistakes, reflect on them, and accept them as you continue to grow.

6. Don't forget about sleep

To do our best work, we need to be well-rested. We all have busy days, but catching up on sleep helps our minds and body. It can be easy to stay up late and push ourselves too hard when our to-do list is full, but this isn't sustainable. Even when you think an extra hour of work will get you closer to your goals, it will likely further exhaust you and harm productivity. Next time this happens, make the mindful choice of sleep. A well-rested body and mind will make you more motivated and ready to start your day.

7. Keep growth in mind

Professional and personal growth is inevitable as you're working towards your goals. Keeping a growth mindset during your journey to success is crucial to remind you of your beginning. If your goals are long-term, take the time and review your progress. Not only will you feel a sense of accomplishment, but you'll be more motivated too. If you're ever discouraged, dividing your goals into several tasks can make your progress feel more tangible. Growth doesn't come overnight and without hard work, which you've done. Thinking about your growth will give you a sense of pride that you should cherish.

8. Stop making excuses for yourself

Excuses will hold you back from pushing forward and achieving your goals. Do you have a problem? Try out some time-tested problem-solving techniques. Try to address problems instead of blaming your setbacks on other factors or complaining. Work with a trusted coach or mentor to understand what is holding you back or causing an issue. Focus on making behavior changes to create change for yourself. Whether that means asking for help, changing your approach, or even taking a break, remember that the worst thing you can do is let your excuses consume you.

9. Learn to invest

When it comes to financial success, the secret of the millionaire's mind is simple: don't lose money. Take your future seriously by prioritizing your financial wellness and setting financial goals that focus on investing over spending. If you need to take financial risks like laying out capital, feel confident the expense will bring returns. Do your research and work closely with successful business people, heeding their advice.

10. Adopt a "now" mentality

While patience is indeed a virtue, one of the habits of wealthy people is jumping at new opportunities. While some of these will mean temporary financial losses, there will also be fewer revenue-based opportunities, such as speaking at events and volunteering to help a startup. The more experiences you have and the more connected you are, the greater your chances of developing personally and professionally.

6 PRO TIPS TO ACHIEVING THE MILLIONAIRE MINDSET

Everyone wants to know the biggest, most effective tips on achieving the millionaire mindset, but the most important tips to keep in mind aren't telling you to buy certain products. They're about honing in on the new lifestyle this mindset brings you.

1. Believe in yourself

The millionaire mindset isn't something you can follow for three days and then reap the benefits forever. It may take more time than you'd hoped. Believe in your ability to reach your goals one day. Remember that you're doing your best, and that's all you can ask for when trying to become the millionaire next door.

2. Be respectful along the way

As you go through this lifestyle change, you're bound to encounter some frustrating times and people. It's okay to feel annoyed or disappointed, but try your best to be as respectful as you can. Once you reach your goals, it'll make you feel more accomplished knowing that you respected everyone who helped you along the way.

3. Turn "I can't" into "I will"

You won't try at something if you don't believe you're capable of doing it. Self-prophesize success by telling yourself you'll achieve your goals as often as possible. Repeat this positive affirmation every day and more often in moments of doubt. And don't let setbacks deter you — you'll achieve your goals, but the road isn't linear.

4. Never trust luck

Confidence and a fantastic career trajectory aren't everything, so always plan for contingencies. Envision worst-case scenarios, create a plan for dealing with them, and work hard to avoid them. For example, times of economic uncertainty mean financial setbacks like layoffs or recession are possible. Save more than your budget requires to ensure you're prepared for anything.

5. Think big!

Creating a clear goal and attributing every daily task to this objective's progress will help you stay motivated and understand why you're working so hard. Remind yourself of this vision when you're feeling stuck or forget your purpose to ignite enthusiasm and energy.

6. Keep love in mind

It's easy to lose sight of what's most important — like your mental health or relationships — when you're working so hard. But your well-being depends on your social health. Research shows that strong social connections are linked to longer life, reduced stress, and improved heart health. Keep friends, family, and coworkers in mind as you work toward your goals. They'll inspire you, you'll encourage them, and this focus on love will propel you forward.

CONCLUSION

Developing a millionaire mindset isn't an overnight process. It involves vision, passion, and an incredible amount of hard work. Have patience and foresight, and know that any setbacks are normal and offer a learning experience.